ULTIMATE CARS

Aston Martin

Rob Scott Colson

WAYLAND

First published in 2009 by Wayland

Copyright © Wayland 2009

Wayland
338 Euston Road
London NW1 3BH

Wayland Australia
Level 17/207 Kent Street
Sydney NSW 2000

Editor: Camilla Lloyd
Produced by Tall Tree Ltd
Editor, Tall Tree: Emma Marriott
Designer: Jonathan Vipond

British Library Cataloguing in Publication Data

Colson, Robert Scott.
   Aston Martin. – (Ultimate cars)
   1. Aston Martin automobile–Juvenile literature.
   I. Title II. Series
   629.2'222-dc22

ISBN: 9780750257244

Printed in China

Wayland is a division of Hachette Children's
Books, an Hachette UK company.

www.hachette.co.uk

Picture credits
Cover main image Shuttlecock/Dreamstime.
com, cover bl Jkt1505/Dreamstime.com, cover br
Featurecars/Dreamstime.com, 1 Motoring Picture
Library/Alamy, 2 Max Earey/Dreamstime.com, 4
Getty Images, 5t Billphilpot/Dreamstime.com, 5b
Pictorial Press Ltd/Alamy, 6 Aude/GNU, 7t Volvo,
7b Bertrand Benoit/Dreamstime.com, 8t Tigrajr/
Dreamstime.com, 8–9 Featurecars/Dreamstime.
com, 9t Aston Martin, 10–11 Zolle/GNU, 11t
Aston Martin, 11b Mark Fosh/GNU, 12 Jeffrey
Keeton/GNU, 13t Tony Hisgett/GNU, 13b Mark
Scheuern/Alamy, 14 Buzz Pictures/Alamy, 15t
Giles Chapman, 15b Mike Dabell/istockphoto, 16
Ed/GNU, 17t Peter Jordan/Alamy, 17b culture-
images GmbH Alamy, 18 Max Earey/Dreamstime.
com, 19t Aude/GNU, 19b Transtock Inc./Alamy,
20 Clemson/GNU sharealike, 21t The359/GNU,
21b Mike Dabell/istockphoto, 24 Zolle/GNU

Contents

Aston Martin

Aston Martin was founded by British racing enthusiasts Lionel Martin and Robert Bamford in 1913. The company has now been making fast cars for almost a century.

The company's name was inspired by Martin's success in 1914 at Aston Clinton, a car race in Buckinghamshire in which drivers raced up Aston Hill. With money from rich backers, Martin and Bamford were soon racing their own cars all around Europe.

Six cars line up at the start of a 100 mile (160 km) race in Surrey, England in 1925. The car second from the left is an Aston Martin Razor Blade.

An Aston Martin International from 1930. The International won many races, including the ultimate endurance race of the time, the Biennial Cup at Le Mans, France, in 1932.

From the track to the road

Racing cars is an expensive business, and by 1947 Aston Martin had run out of money. They were saved by David Brown, who bought the company and started production of a series of models known as DB, named after his initials. The DB series was successful both on the race track and in the showroom. It established Aston Martin as a manufacturer of stylish high-performance sports cars.

Amazing design

Movie secret agent James Bond was first seen behind the wheel of an Aston Martin in the 1964 movie *Goldfinger*. Bond has driven an Aston Martin in eight films since then, and drives the new DBS in the 2008 movie *Quantum of Solace*. Aston Martin's long association with the Bond films has made the car famous around the world.

Bond makes his escape in an Aston Martin Vanquish in the movie Die Another Day.

DB9

The DB9 is a 'grand tourer', which means that it is a fast car designed to be driven over long distances.

Its powerful engine is controlled by a computer – a system known as 'drive-by-wire'. When the driver wants to change gear, they move the gear stick. This sends a message to the computer, which makes the change. On long journeys, the driver can switch to automatic and let the computer decide when to change gear.

The DB9 Volante is a convertible, which means that its roof can be taken off on a sunny day.

Shaped for speed

To reach its top speed of over 300 kph, the DB9 needs to be as aerodynamic as possible. This means that its shape must allow air to flow smoothly over it. Aston Martin tested different shapes in a wind tunnel, where air was blown over models to see what would happen to them. The shape they came up with makes the car look like it is pointing in the direction it wants to go!

STATS AND FACTS

YEARS OF PRODUCTION **2003–present**
ENGINE SIZE **6 litre**
NUMBER OF CYLINDERS **12**
TRANSMISSION **Manual/Automatic**
GEARBOX **6-speed**
0–100 KPH (0–62 MPH) **4.8 seconds**
TOP SPEED **306 kph**
WEIGHT (KG) **1760**
CO_2 EMISSIONS (G/KM) **394**
FUEL ECONOMY (L/100 KM) **16.5 (17.1 mpg)**

Amazing design

A car is crashed to check its safety at Volvo's testing centre.

You might think that a car would be safest if it were strong all over. But the front and rear of the DB9 are designed to crumple up in a collision. These are known as crumple zones. They absorb the impact, protecting the passengers who sit inside a very strong 'cell' in the middle. Aston Martin developed their crumple zones at Volvo's testing centre in Sweden, where cars are crashed with test dummies inside.

The DB9 Coupé has a fixed roof. It is lighter and faster than the Volante.

7

V8 Vantage

Smaller than the DB9, the V8 Vantage is still a powerful eight-cylinder car, and its size makes it easier to handle at high speeds. It can take corners at well over 100 kph if you are brave enough to try it.

Like all Aston Martins, the V8 Vantage is hand-built in small numbers. Just 3,000 are made each year. If you want one, you'd better get your name down soon as there is a long waiting list!

The coupé is a hatchback, which gives it more room in the boot for storage.

Hard or soft top

Customers can choose a hard-top coupé or a soft-top roadster. In the coupé, the whole of the back lifts up to get into the boot. This is known as a hatchback. The roadster uses much of its boot space to fold away the soft roof. The roadster's body is reinforced (made stronger) to make up for not having a hard roof. This makes it heavier and slower than the coupé.

A computer screen shows the car's location, which is worked out by communicating with satellites – a system known as Sat Nav.

The digital display shows what music is playing.

Amazing design

The V8 Vantage's luxury fittings have been taken from the DB9. The leather seats are hand-stitched, and this old-world style is matched with the latest technology. You can plug your own iPod into its music system, which is controlled by the driver from the steering wheel so that the hands can remain safely in control of the car.

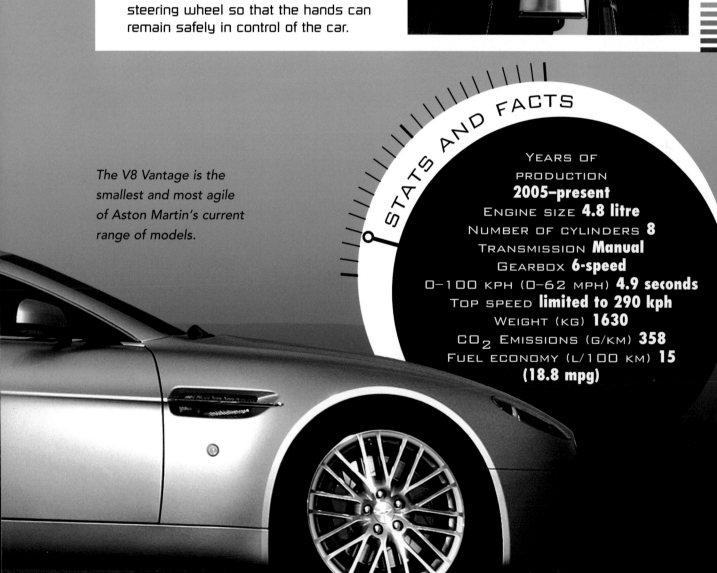

The V8 Vantage is the smallest and most agile of Aston Martin's current range of models.

STATS AND FACTS

YEARS OF PRODUCTION **2005–present**
ENGINE SIZE **4.8 litre**
NUMBER OF CYLINDERS **8**
TRANSMISSION **Manual**
GEARBOX **6-speed**
0–100 KPH (0–62 MPH) **4.9 seconds**
TOP SPEED **limited to 290 kph**
WEIGHT (KG) **1630**
CO_2 EMISSIONS (G/KM) **358**
FUEL ECONOMY (L/100 KM) **15 (18.8 mpg)**

DBS

The DBS is the fastest road-legal Aston Martin of all. It has the same engine as the DB9, but its body is very light, which allows it to go even faster.

The driver can choose a standard set-up for comfort or sport set-up with a stiffer suspension. With the sport set-up, you feel every bump, but it makes the car more responsive and even more exciting to drive.

STATS AND FACTS

YEARS OF PRODUCTION
2007–present
ENGINE SIZE **6 litre**
NUMBER OF CYLINDERS **12**
TRANSMISSION **Manual/semi automatic**
GEARBOX **6-speed**
0–100 KPH (0–62 MPH) **4.3 seconds**
TOP SPEED **307 kph**
WEIGHT (KG) **1695**
CO_2 EMISSIONS (G/KM) **388**
FUEL ECONOMY (L/100 KM)
16.4 (17.2 mpg)

Amazing design

The handmade V12 engine is fine-tuned to extract maximum power. When the engine is roaring at full speed, its pistons pump over 5,500 times a minute (known as revolutions per minute or rpm). At this rate, more air needs to be taken into the engine so that the fuel burns properly. A 'by-pass' air intake opens automatically at 5,500 rpm to make sure there is enough air at all times.

The engine is at the front, but set back towards the middle to make the car balanced.

Movie magic

The first time the world saw the DBS was in the Bond film *Casino Royale* in 2006. The car was still in development during filming, so two fake cars were specially made for the close-ups. The stunts were performed in old DB9s that had been made up to look like the DBS from the outside. A world-record of 7½ rolls was set in one stunt. At first the stunt drivers could not get the cars to roll at all, because they were so stable.

The body of the DBS looks like it is made from shiny metal, but is in fact lightweight carbon fibre.

The weight of the DBS is distributed evenly across the car, which makes it very stable.

DBR9

The DBR9 is designed for endurance races, in which cars complete as many laps of a track as they can in a set number of hours.

The car's chassis (its 'skeleton') is the same as the DB9's, but the DBR9 is a much lighter car. The body panels are lightweight carbon fibre and inside the luxury features have been removed to save weight.

A DBR9 in one of the first races it entered – the 2005 Petit Le Mans, held in Georgia, USA. It finished fourth.

STATS AND FACTS

Years of production **2005–present**
Engine size **6 litre**
Number of cylinders **12**
Transmission **Sequential**
Gearbox **6-speed**
0–100 kph (0–62 mph) **3.5 seconds**
Top speed **300 kph**
Weight (kg) **1100**
CO_2 Emissions (g/km) **Not available**
Fuel economy (l/100 km)
Not available

Le Mans

The most important endurance race is the 24-hour Le Mans, a race in France where teams of drivers drive a car continuously for a whole day. It is really four races in one, as cars are divided into different 'classes' according to the kind of car they are. The DBR9 won the GT1 class for large grand tourers in 2007 and 2008. It can now claim to be the best grand tourer in the world.

British racing driver Johnny Herbert shows off some moves in the DBR9 that won the 2007 Le Mans GT1 class.

spoiler

rear airflow splitter

Amazing design

The most visible difference between the DBR9 and road cars is its huge rear spoiler. The body of the car allows air to flow around it, but the spoiler disrupts the air flow at the back. Instead of flowing smoothly, the air pushes the spoiler down. This gives the car better grip, which allows it to take corners more quickly. The spoiler reduces the car's top speed, but it is the speed around corners that wins races on bendy tracks.

DB5

The DB5 cannot match modern-day Aston Martins for performance, but was one of the fastest cars on the road in the 1960s.

It was built using the most advanced technology of its time. Its body is made of a light mix of metals called an alloy, and its engine of light aluminium. It was much lighter than other cars of the same size and could reach speeds of well over 200 kph.

STATS AND FACTS

YEARS OF PRODUCTION **1963–1965**
ENGINE SIZE **4 litre**
NUMBER OF CYLINDERS **6**
TRANSMISSION **Manual**
GEARBOX **5-speed**
0–100 KPH (0–62 MPH) **7.2 seconds**
TOP SPEED **limited to 238 kph**
WEIGHT (KG) **1465**
CO_2 EMISSIONS (G/KM)
Not available
FUEL ECONOMY (L/100 KM)
Not available

A DB5 Coupé. It also came as a convertible.

Just 12 shooting-brake DB5s were ever made. This one was used to carry medics and their supplies.

Amazing design

A limited number of DB5s were specially designed with a squared-off rear and a hatchback boot, known as a 'shooting-brake' estate car. They are named after the long horse-drawn carriages used to carry hunters and their guns in the 19th century. The shooting-brake DB5 was more likely to have a set of golf clubs or polo sticks in the back!

The first Bond car

A test model of the DB5, known as a prototype, was used in the Bond film *Goldfinger*. James Bond had some extras in his car that other drivers were not offered. These included machine guns behind each front light, a bullet-proof rear window, and an oil sprayer in the rear lights to make the road slippery for anyone chasing him.

The rear lights of the specially adapted Bond car folded down from the top to reveal an oil sprayer.

DB7

More than 7,000 DB7s were made between 1994 and 2003, making it the most successful Aston Martin model ever.

It replaced the Aston Martin V8, a car that had been in production for more than 20 years. The DB7 had a much more sleek and aerodynamic design than the V8 and put new life into the company, which had been losing money.

A changing design

The first DB7s were coupés with six-cylinder engines. They were smaller and cheaper than the old V8. In 1997, a convertible model called the DB7 Volante was made. Then in 1999, the car was refitted with a 12-cylinder engine. Known as the DB7 Vantage, the new car could go 32 kph faster than the six-cylinder models, and was an instant hit. The 'Stats and Facts' opposite are for the DB7 Vantage.

The DB7 Volante was first shown at the 1996 International Auto Show in Detroit, USA, and went on sale a year later.

The DB7 production line in Kidlington, Oxfordshire, where the car was assembled for Aston Martin by the company TWR.

STATS AND FACTS

Years of production **2000–2003**
Engine size **6 litre**
Number of cylinders **12**
Transmission **Manual**
Gearbox **5-speed**
0–100 kph (0–62 mph) **5 seconds**
Top speed **298 kph**
Weight (kg) **1780**
CO_2 Emissions (g/km) **Not available**
Fuel economy (l/100 km) **15.7 (18mpg)**

Amazing design

When they were developing the DB7, Aston Martin wanted to make sure it would be a strong car that could be driven anywhere. They made 30 prototypes and test-drove them in the most extreme conditions of hot and cold they could find around the world. In total, more than 800,000 km were driven testing the DB7. That's as far as driving to the Moon and back!

The engine in the V12 Vantage is nearly twice the capacity of that in the original DB7.

Vanquish

From 2001–2007, the Vanquish was Aston Martin's flagship model – the fastest, most luxurious car they made.

The Vanquish was the last car to be made at the factory in Newport Pagnell, where traditional methods were used, such as hand-beating the body panels into shape. The company uses more modern methods at its new plant in nearby Gaydon, where cars are built in half the time.

The Vanquish is due to be replaced by a new, even more powerful model in 2010.

The wheels of the Vanquish S are made from a light metal alloy to keep weight to a minimum.

Amazing design

In 2004, a sporty model called the Vanquish S was produced, fitted with a redesigned engine. The new model could produce a maximum power of 520 brake horse power (bhp), an increase of 60 bhp over the old model. The Vanquish S had special sporty settings to take advantage of this extra power, with a stiffer suspension and more responsive steering. It makes for a bumpy but thrilling ride.

Paddle to change gear

STATS AND FACTS

YEARS OF PRODUCTION **2001–2007**
ENGINE SIZE **5.9 litre**
NUMBER OF CYLINDERS **12**
TRANSMISSION **Sequential manual**
GEARBOX **6-speed**
0–100 KPH (0–62 MPH) **4.4 seconds**
TOP SPEED **315 kph**
WEIGHT (KG) **1835**
CO_2 EMISSIONS (G/KM) **396**
FUEL ECONOMY (L/100 KM)
16.7 (16.9 mpg)

Computer control

To change gear, drivers usually use the clutch to disconnect the engine from the wheels. This causes a temporary loss of power. In the Vanquish, the clutch is operated by a computer, and the driver changes up or down a gear using a paddle on the steering wheel. This reduces the power loss and is the system used in Formula 1 cars.

Racing models

The Aston Martin company began its life making racing cars, and success on the track has always been very important to them.

Up to the 1950s, they had a great deal of success, but their fortunes went into decline in the 1960s. In recent years, they have returned to their winning ways. The DBRS started racing in 2004, twice winning the GT1 class for large grand tourers at Le Mans. In 2008, the new Vantage GT2 was entered into its first race. In future years it is expected to challenge in the GT2 class for smaller grand tourers at Le Mans. Aston Martin are back with a winning roar.

The Vantage GT2 made its racing debut at the 2008 American Le Mans Series at Long Beach, California, where it was driven by British drivers Paul Drayson and Johnny Cocker.

Victory at Le Mans

When David Brown bought Aston Martin in 1947, his dream was to win the 24-hour Le Mans. Twelve years later, his dream came true. Aston Martin entered two DBR1s in the race and they came home first and second, 25 laps ahead of the third-placed car. It is the only time Aston Martin have ever won overall victory at Le Mans, although they have won individual class categories. The DBR1's Stats and Facts are listed below.

A DBR1 in action at a race for classic cars at Silverstone, England, in 2007.

STATS AND FACTS

Years of production **1956–1959 (just 5 built)**
Engine size **3 litre**
Number of cylinders **6**
Transmission **Manual**
Gearbox **5-speed**
0–100 kph (0–62 mph) **Not available**
Top speed **280 kph**
Weight (kg) **800**
CO_2 Emissions (g/km) **Not available**
Fuel economy (l/100 km) **Not available**

In the 1960s, the DB4 GT Zagato was raced at Le Mans, but it was unable to reproduce the success of the DBR1.

Glossary

aerodynamic
Shaped to minimize air resistance when moving at high speed.

air intake
A hole in the outside of the car that allows air in when the car is moving. This air is used in the car's cooling system.

carbon fibre
A lightweight modern material often used instead of metal.

chassis
The frame or skeleton of the car to which the body and the engine are attached.

clutch
A means of disconnecting the engine from the wheels in order to change gear.

coupé
A car with a hard roof that cannot be removed.

crumple zone
Part of a car that is designed to collapse in a crash, protecting passengers from the full force of the impact.

drive-by-wire
Where a computer controls actions such as changing gear or putting fuel into the engine.

endurance race
A race in which cars are driven as far as they can within a set time limit.

fuel economy
The rate at which a car uses fuel. It is measured in litres per 100 kilometres or miles per gallon.

gear
A system of cogs that control the transfer of power from the engine to the wheels. Low gears give extra power for acceleration or driving uphill. High gears are used for driving at faster speeds.

grand tourer
A sports car that is designed to be driven long distances.

performance
A measurement of a car's power and handling.

prototype
An experimental model made to test a design before it goes into production.

piston
A metal rod that pumps up and down inside a cylinder to produce an engine's power.

suspension
A system of springs and shock absorbers that makes the ride smoother as the wheels pass over bumps.

transmission
The way in which a car transfers power from the engine to the wheels, via a gearbox that allows the driver to change gear.

Models at a glance

Model	Years Made	Numbers Built	Did You Know?
DB1	1948–50	15	It was originally called the Aston Martin 2-Litre Sports, and only became known as the DB1 in 1950.
DBR1	1956–59	5	The DBR1 was only built for racing. It would have been illegal to drive one on a normal road.
DB5	1964–65	1,021	It appeared in five James Bond films. In *Goldfinger*, two cars were used – one for close-ups and one for stunts.
DB7	1994–2003	7,000	When the Vantage was brought out, nobody wanted to buy the original DB7, so they stopped making it.
Vanquish	2001–07	2,578	The Vanquish's powerful V12 engine was designed by Ford Research in the United States.
DB9	2004–present	4,000 per year	A built-in computer constantly checks the engine in the DB9 to make sure it is running smoothly.
V8 Vantage	2005–present	3,000 per year	The leather interior of the V8 Vantage is entirely hand-stitched.
DBR9	2005–present	32	The company runs a team with 12 DBR9s in a new division known as Aston Martin Racing.
DBS	2007–present	The company plans to build 300	In February 2009, Aston Martin announced on Facebook that it was making a convertible DBS Volante.

Websites

www.astonmartin.com

Aston Martin's official website with info and images of their latest models plus features on the company's history and their most famous models from the past.

www.amoc.org

The website of the Aston Martin Owners' Club. It features a fascinating section listing every model made since the company began in 1914.

www.astonmartins.com

An interesting site, with photos and reviews of Aston Martins through the ages.

www.topgear.com

Top Gear, the popular BBC TV series, has an excellent website, with reviews and clips from the show. The presenters say what they love, and also what they hate, about the newest Aston Martins.

Index

Contents of titles in series:

WAYLAND